Haley Helps at School

Use Place Value and Properties of Operations to Add

Blaine Fronczak

New York

Published in 2014 by The Rosen Publishing Group, Inc.
29 East 21st Street, New York, NY 10010

Copyright © 2014 by The Rosen Publishing Group, Inc.

All rights reserved. No part of this book may be reproduced in any form without permission in writing from the publisher, except by a reviewer.

Book Design: Katelyn Londino

Photo Credits: Cover, pp. 5, 7, 9, 11, 22 Monkey Business Images/Shutterstock.com; p. 13 Christopher Hall/Shutterstock.com; p. 15 hxdbzxy/Shutterstock.com; p. 17 iStockphoto/Thinkstock.com; p. 19 Doug Martin/Photo Researchers/Getty Images; p. 21 Sergii Figurnyi/Shutterstock.com.

Library of Congress Cataloging-in-Publication Data

Fronczak, Blaine.
Haley helps at school : use place value and properties of operations to add / Blaine Fronczak.
    pages cm — (Core math skills: Numbers and operations in base 10)
Includes index.
ISBN 978-1-4777-2097-4 (paperback)
ISBN 978-1-4777-2098-1 (6-pack)
ISBN 978-1-4777-2225-1 (library binding)
1. Addition—Juvenile literature. 2. Place value (Mathematics)—Juvenile literature. 3. Helping behavior—Juvenile literature. 4. Schools—Juvenile literature. I. Title.
QA115.F765 2013
513.2'11—dc23
                              2013007600

Manufactured in the United States of America

CPSIA Compliance Information: Batch #CS13RC: For further information contact Rosen Publishing, New York, New York at 1-800-237-9932.

Word Count: 455

Contents

Helping Is Fun!	4
How Many Students?	6
Art Projects	8
Lunchtime!	14
The Classroom Library	16
Feeding the Fish	18
A Good Helper	22
Glossary	23
Index	24

Helping Is Fun!

Haley loves school. She likes to help her teacher, Mrs. Rubio, with jobs around the classroom. Haley's friends like to help at school, too. Helping at school can be lots of fun!

How Many Students?

There are 10 boys and 10 girls in Haley's class. Haley can add to see how many students are in her class altogether. First, she adds the numbers in the ones place. Then, she adds the numbers in the tens place. When she puts the tens and ones together, she gets 20!

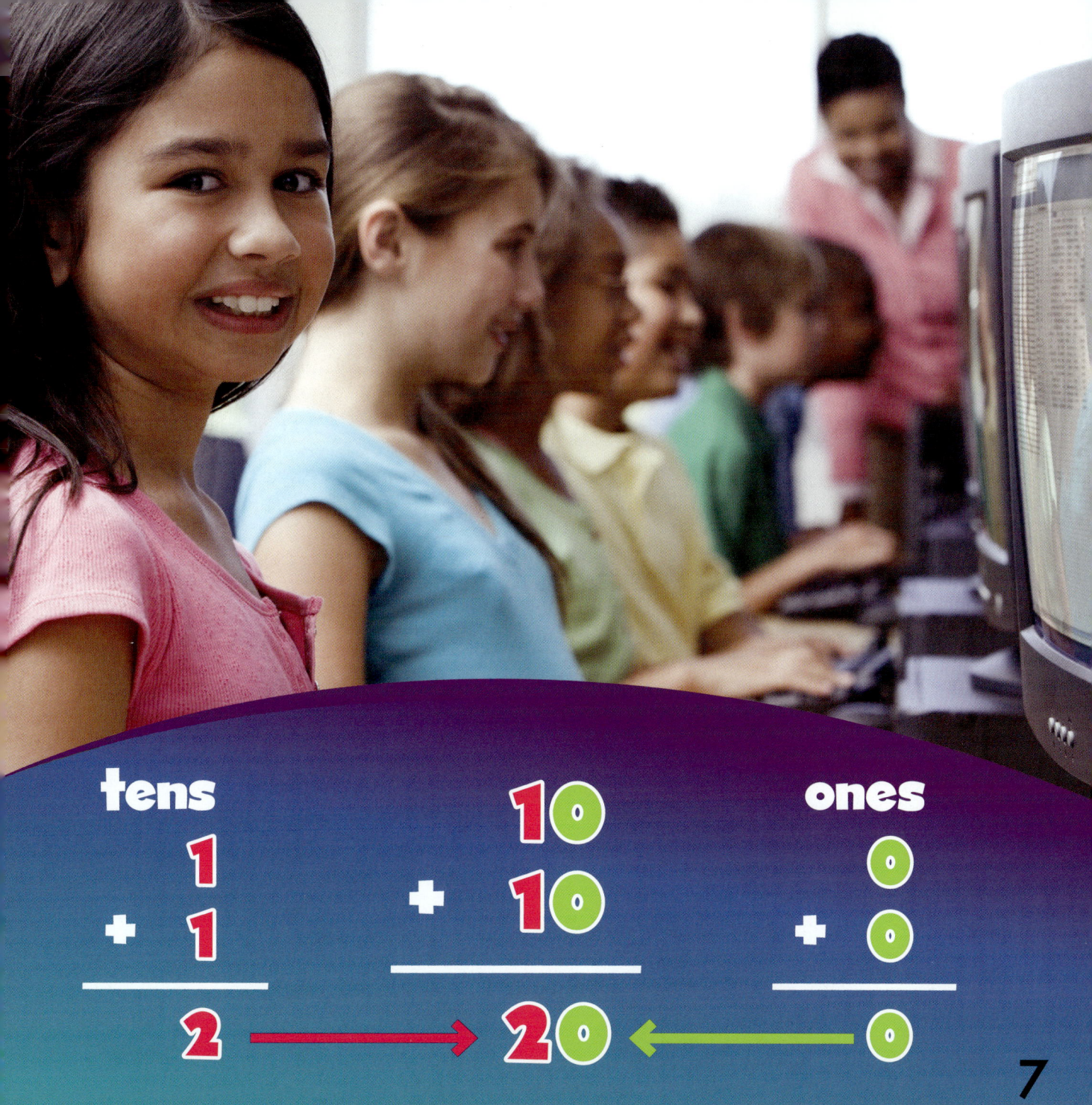

Art Projects

Haley helps Mrs. Rubio pass out paper for an art **project**. She passes out 11 big pieces of paper and 13 small ones. Haley adds the numbers in the ones place first to make 4. Then, she adds the numbers in the tens place to make 2. That makes 24 pieces of paper!

Haley's friend Marco passes out markers for the class to use. He has 14 red markers and 15 blue markers. Haley uses math to find out how many markers he has. First, she adds 4 and 5 to get 9 ones. Then she adds 1 and 1 to get 2 tens. Marco has 29 markers altogether.

Mrs. Rubio gives Haley's class star stickers to use on their art projects. Haley passes out 23 silver stars and 34 gold stars. First, Haley adds 3 and 4 to make 7 ones. Then, she adds 2 and 3 to make 5 tens. She knows there are 57 star stickers altogether.

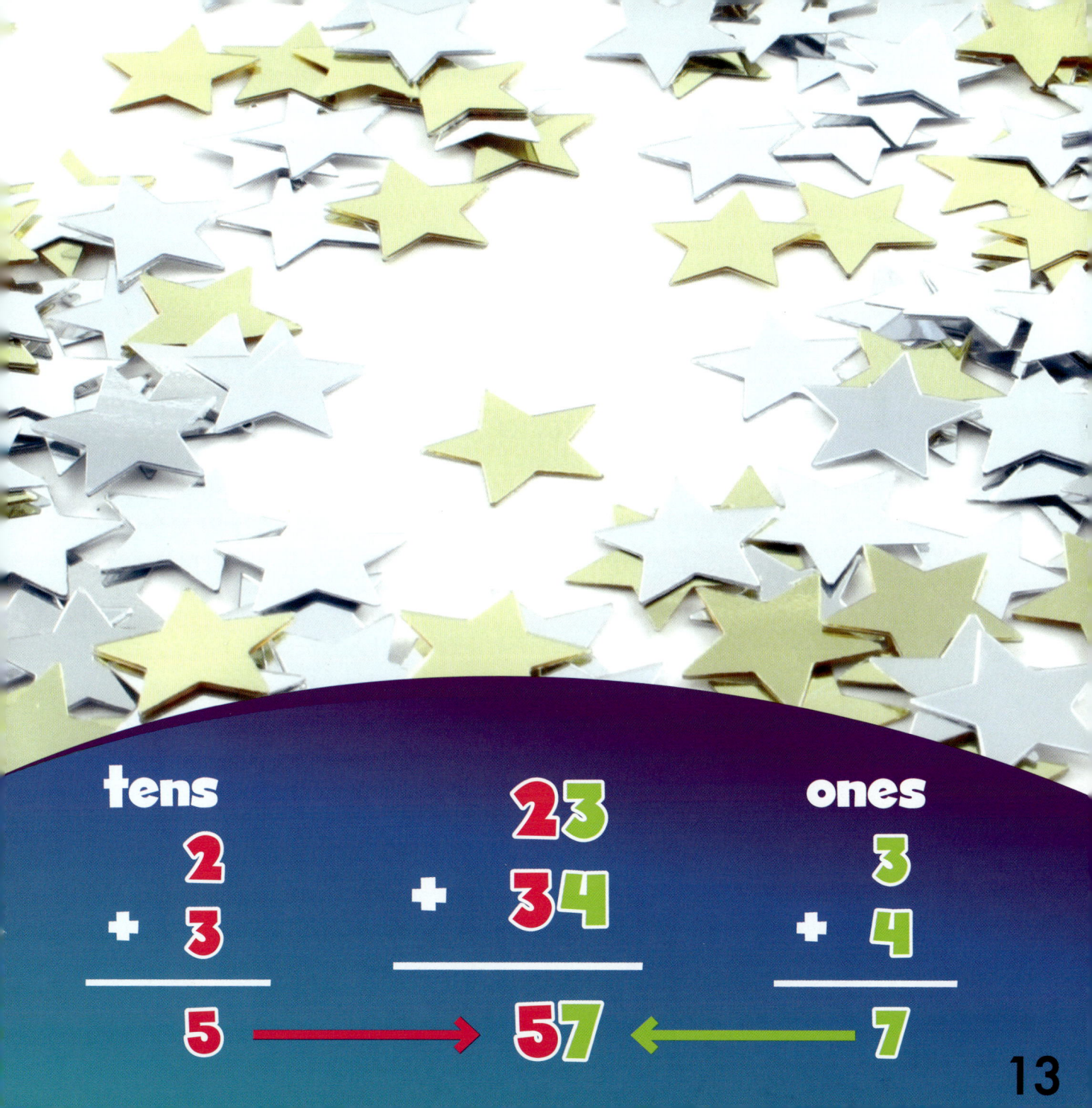

Lunchtime!

After lunch, Haley and her friend Maddie push in the chairs in the **cafeteria**. Haley pushes in 17 chairs. Maddie pushes in 12 chairs. They add the 7 and 2 to get 9 ones. Then, they add the 1 and 1 to get 2 tens. Together, they push in 29 chairs.

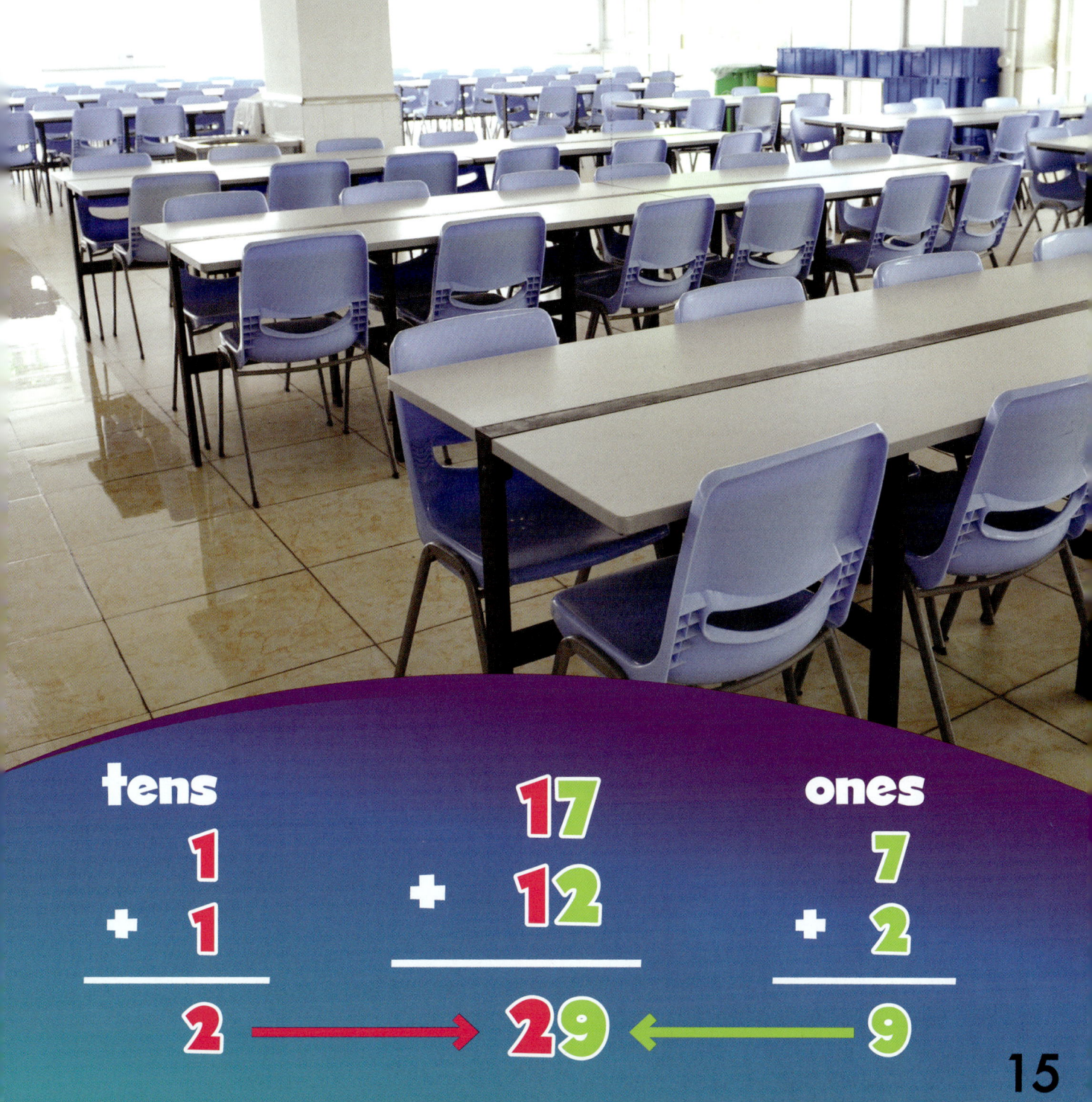

The Classroom Library

Haley likes to help Mrs. Rubio clean up the classroom **library**. On Monday, she puts away 16 books. On Tuesday, she puts away 10 books. Haley knows she put away 26 books altogether. First, she adds 6 and 0 to make 6 ones. Then, she adds 1 and 1 to make 2 tens.

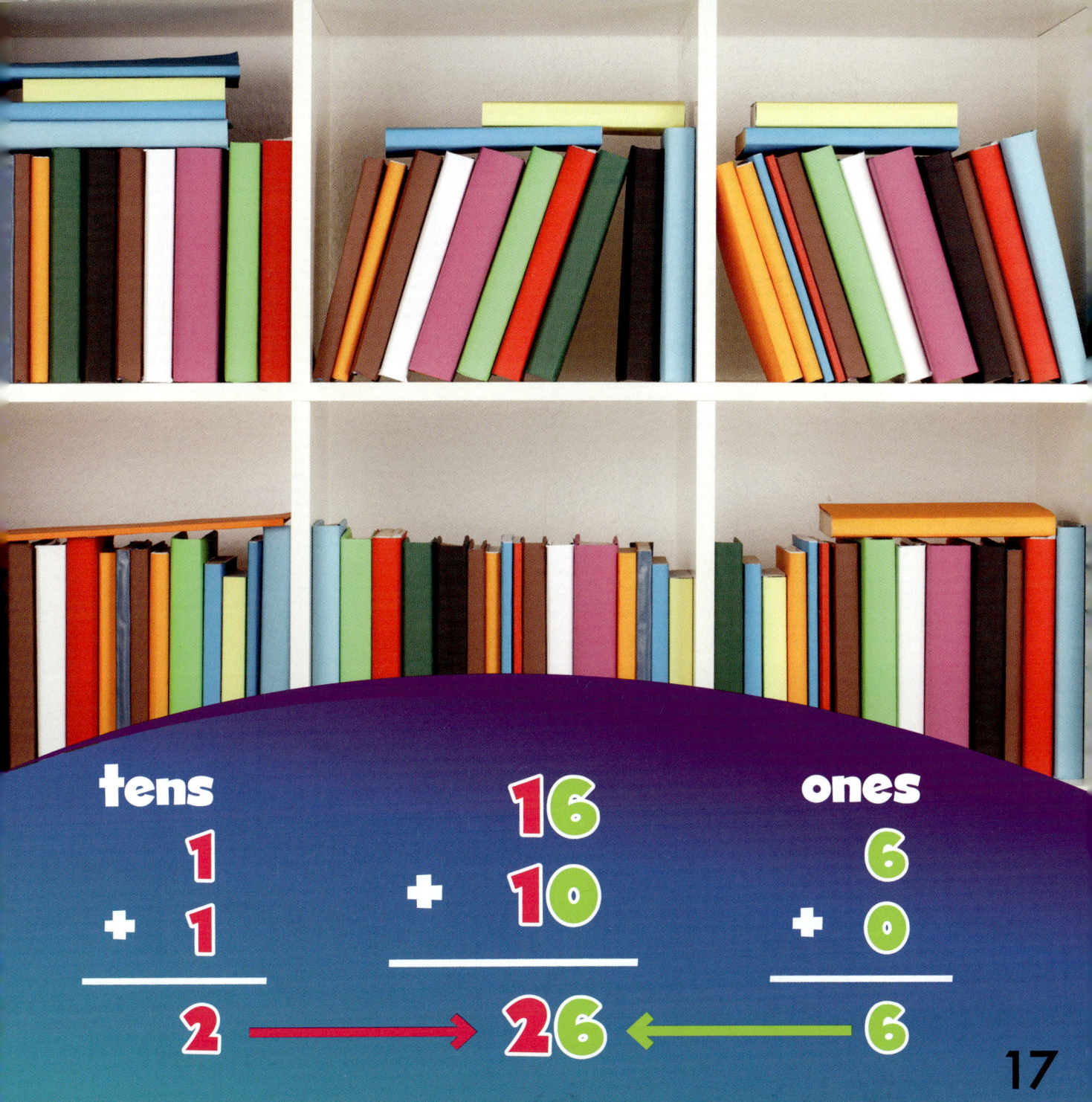

Feeding the Fish

Haley's classroom has a big fish **tank**! There are many kinds of little fish that swim in the tank. Haley likes to feed the fish. Her friend Tyson has a fish tank in his classroom, too.

Haley counts the fish in the tank as she feeds them. There are 20 fish in her classroom fish tank. Tyson's fish tank has 11 fish in it. How many fish are in the 2 tanks altogether? Which numbers should Haley and Tyson add first to find out?

A Good Helper

Haley has fun helping Mrs. Rubio and other people around her school. She knows she's doing something nice by being a good helper.

cafeteria (kaa-fuh-TIHR-ee-uh) A room in a school used for eating.

library (LY-brehr-ee) A place where books are kept to be read and borrowed.

project (PRAH-jehkt) A task.

tank (TANK) Something that holds water and is often a home for fish.

Index

art project(s), 8, 12
books, 16
cafeteria, 14
chairs, 14
class, 6, 10, 12
classroom, 4, 16, 18, 20
fish, 18, 20
fish tank, 18, 20
library, 16
markers, 10

paper, 8
star stickers, 12
students, 6
teacher, 4

Due to the changing nature of Internet links, The Rosen Publishing Group, Inc., has developed an online list of websites related to the subject of this book. This site is updated regularly. Please use this link to access the list: www.powerkidslinks.com/cms/nob/hhs